I0529228

SOUL
of a
LEADER

A Guidebook to Uncovering
Who You Are

THOMAS WHITE

STILLPOINT
MEDIA

Copyright © 2025 Thomas White
All rights reserved. No part of this book may be reproduced in any
form by any electronic or mechanical means without permission in
writing from the author except in the case of brief quotations used in
critical articles, reviews, and scholarly works.

Published by Stillpoint Media, LLC

ISBN: 979-8-9900584-3-9

Cover design: Nicholas Tippins and SHR Book Design
Interior design: SHR Book Design

To the leader within you awaiting your discovery

Table of Contents

Preface

THIS IS NOT A BOOK ABOUT LEADERSHIP. THIS IS a book about remembering.

It will not teach you how to lead, or what to say, or which mountain to climb. It will not hand you blueprints or mantras or frameworks.

Instead, it will sit with you at the edge of your own silence and wait until you remember that you already know.

The soul does not need to be trained. It needs to be trusted.

In these pages, you will not be asked to become someone else. You will not be asked to fix, to prove, to perform. You will only be invited to return—to the still, unshaken ground of who you already are.

The world is loud with instruction. This book is quiet with invitation.

It is written not from belief, but from knowing—that leadership is not a role you step into, but a radiance that steps out of you when you stop pretending.

There is no urgency here. No race. There is only rhythm. Forgetting and remembering. Unraveling and resting. A homecoming, again and again.

You are not late. You have not missed anything. Everything in you belongs.

As you turn these pages, may you feel what's always been true: That your presence is enough. That truth does not shout. That what leads the world best is what listens most deeply.

Welcome back. We've been waiting.

Introduction

Why Leadership Begins with Being, Not Doing

YOU HAVE LIKELY BEEN TOLD THAT LEADERSHIP is something you earn. That it arrives after proving, after preparation, after the right performance. You've likely been handed tools, techniques, frameworks—ways to do it "right." But perhaps something deeper in you has always known: this is not it.

Leadership does not begin with action. It begins with attention. With being. With a felt sense that you are not here to become more—but to uncover what has always been.

This book is not a manual. It is not a performance guide. It is a companion for the rhythm all souls know: remembering, forgetting, remembering again. It is a mirror held not to your image, but to your essence.

You are not being prepared for leadership. You are being reminded you are already a leader.

Not because you hold power. But because you are willing to hold presence. Not because others follow you. But because you no longer abandon yourself.

I did not write this book because I mastered something. I wrote it because I, too, am remembering. Every chapter is a stepping stone back to what I've always known but often forget. And in writing it, I am inviting you—not as student, not as follower, but as fellow traveler—to join me in this unfolding.

This book is written from knowing. Knowing that the soul of a leader is not built by effort, but revealed by stillness. Knowing that truth is not a possession, but a resonance. Knowing that there is nothing more magnetic than someone rooted in what's real.

The pages ahead will not give you answers. They will ask you to listen. They will not fix you. They will remind you: *there is nothing to fix.* You are not an image to be improved. You are a living expression of something already whole.

Leadership, then, is not a task. It is a return. A return to coherence. To clarity. To the subtle, luminous frequency of truth.

You are the leader. You are the audience. You are the guide.

Let us begin.

1 The Loop of Forgetting and Remembering

The rhythm beneath the illusion of progress

> *The journey of a thousand miles begins with one step.*
> —Lao Tzu

WE ARE TAUGHT TO SEE TIME as a line.
Forward motion. Upward progress.
As if growth is something we chase, something we earn,
something just beyond where we are now.

But the soul doesn't move in lines.
It moves in loops.

You remember.
You forget.
You remember again.

This is not a mistake in the system.
It *is* the system.

There's a moment—you've felt it—
when all the noise falls away and you're simply ... here.
No grasping. No trying.
Just a quiet clarity, as if the sky inside you cleared.

And then—without warning—you forget.
Life rushes in. Doubt. Distraction. The mind resumes
its commentary.
You're back in the loop.

But forgetting isn't failure.
It's the breath between the knowing.
It's not that truth disappears—it's that our gaze wanders.

The soul never forgets.
Only attention does.

Truth doesn't vanish. It waits.

Truth is not fragile.
It doesn't leave because you looked away.
It doesn't resent being forgotten.

It simply waits—like a moon behind passing clouds.
Still full. Still shining.
Still there.

The forgetting is sacred, too.

We've been conditioned to panic in the forgetting.
To assume we've lost something. Slipped backward.
But what if forgetting isn't a detour—it's a deepening?

Forgetting softens us.
It humbles the sharp edges of certainty.
It opens us to wonder again.

And when remembering comes, it lands more fully.
Not because we worked harder—but because we let go
more gently.

This loop—the forgetting and remembering—is not a sign
you're broken.
It's a spiral of return.

Each time, you come back to yourself more wholly.
Each time, the remembering roots a little deeper.

You don't need to hold onto truth.
You only need to return to it.

Again.
And again.
And again.

This is the rhythm of awakening.

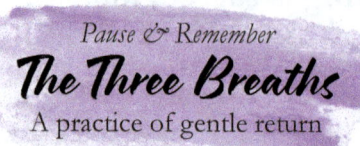

Pause & Remember

The Three Breaths
A practice of gentle return

First breath:
Let it come to you. Don't pull. Receive.
Feel where your attention has wandered. No judgment.

Second breath:
Let it move through your body.
Ask, softly: *What have I forgotten?*
Let the question settle.

Third breath:
Exhale without effort.
Let go of needing to grasp this moment.
Trust that return is always available.

You don't need more time.
You don't need more clarity.
You only need to pause and remember:

You are already home.

———

Tell me, what is it you plan to do with
your one wild and precious life?
—Mary Oliver

2 The Illusion of Identity

Who are you when you stop performing?

> *The only lasting truth is change.*
> *God is change.*
> —Octavia E. Butler

WE ALL WEAR NAMES.

Roles. Titles. Traits we've been told or chosen to wear.

We say, *I am this. I am that.*

But so often, what we call identity is really just memory—with emotions attached.

We think we are the self that others reflect back to us.

We shape ourselves to be approved, applauded, accepted.

We become good at being what we think is lovable.

And without noticing, we begin to perform a self.

We live inside costumes we forgot we put on.

This isn't a flaw.

It's a survival song.

A way of finding belonging in a world that rewards the familiar over the true.

But there comes a moment—a quiet, aching moment—when performance begins to feel like confinement.
When the mask grows too heavy.
When we long not to be impressive, but real.

The self as belief, not being

Most of what we call identity is not who we are.
It's what we've come to believe about who we are.

Belief is sticky.
It wraps itself around experience, tells a story, and repeats it until it feels like truth.

But belief is not knowing.
And identity, when built on belief, becomes a house of mirrors—endlessly reflecting, never revealing.

You are not your roles.
Not your résumé.
Not the story someone told you about yourself in childhood, or last week, or yesterday.

You are not even the version of yourself you've worked hard to curate.

You are what remains when the story pauses.
You are what watches the performance—and knows it is a performance.

The Illusion of Identity

Identity is art, not armor.

What if identity isn't meant to be fixed?
What if it's meant to be fluid—like breath, like water, like light?

You can shape it. Color it. Embody it for a while.
But you don't have to defend it. You don't have to become
trapped by it.

When identity becomes armor, it cuts you off—from others,
from change, from the deeper intelligence moving through
you.

But when identity becomes art, it liberates.
It becomes expression, not protection.
Play, not pressure.
Truth, not branding.

You are allowed to change.
You are allowed to not know who you are sometimes.
You are allowed to stop performing and simply be.

Leadership begins there.
Not with authority. But with authenticity.
Not with charisma. But with coherence.

Who are you without your roles?

This is not a question to answer quickly.
It is one to sit with.
Let it open something in you.

Who are you without the need to be perceived a certain way?
Who are you when you stop trying to prove you are enough?
Who are you when you stop rehearsing your life and begin inhabiting it?

You may not have words for it yet.
The deepest truths aren't always linguistic. They're felt.
Like a loosening in the chest.
Like an exhale after years of holding in.

Sit somewhere quietly.
Close your eyes if you wish.
Ask yourself, *Who am I performing for today?*

Notice what roles are active.
The parent. The professional. The one who has it all together.
Don't judge. Just see.

Now, softly ask:
What would remain if I didn't need to be any of that?
You don't need an answer. Just let the question breathe.

Let yourself feel into the space behind identity.
The stillness. The presence.
The part of you that simply *is*.

Stay there, even for a moment.
Leadership begins here.

*The privilege of a lifetime is to become
who you truly are.*

—Carl Jung

幻

Illusion

3 *The Pause before Action*

The still point in the cycle

> The Tao never acts, yet nothing is left undone.
>
> —Lao Tzu

WE ARE TAUGHT TO VALUE MOMENTUM.
To keep going. Keep producing. Keep moving.
As if speed confirms purpose.
As if urgency equals importance.

But action without alignment becomes noise.
And momentum without meaning becomes escape.

There is a moment—often ignored, often dismissed—
when the soul calls for stillness.
A pause.
Not to retreat from life, but to return to yourself.

This is the space between knowing and doing.
Between sensing and choosing.
Between the inner shift and the outer step.

This is the pause before action.

Listening before leading

Leadership doesn't begin with initiative.
It begins with listening.

Not to others. Not yet.
But to the deeper current moving through you.

The part of you that knows what is right before the mind
makes it reasonable.
The part that doesn't rush.
That doesn't need proof.
That simply knows.

When you pause long enough to listen, something ancient and
immediate emerges.
Not a strategy.
Not a reaction.
But a clear sense of: *This is what's true right now.*

That knowing—quiet, grounded, non-negotiable—becomes
your compass.
Not because it's perfect, but because it's real.

Discerning truth from momentum

Not all movement is alignment.
Not all action is integrity.
Sometimes, what looks like productivity is just avoidance
wearing a suit.

When we move too quickly, we mistake momentum for clarity.
We react instead of respond.
We chase instead of choose.

The pause is not resistance.
It is remembering.

It is a way of asking, *Is this true? Or just familiar?*
Is this action a reflection of who I am, or a reflex from who I've been
taught to be?

In this pause, clarity has room to rise.
Not forced. Not fabricated.
But felt.

The power of sacred interruption

The pause is a sacred interruption.
It breaks the trance of performance.
It creates a gap wide enough for awareness to enter.

In that gap, truth often whispers something surprising:
You don't have to do anything right now.
You are allowed to be before you act.

This is not passivity.
It's power.

The power to act from wholeness instead of compulsion.
To speak from knowing rather than reaction.
To lead from depth instead of speed.

You are not here to be efficient.
You are here to be in rhythm with what is real.

The pause is the beginning of that rhythm.
It is the portal between intention and impact.

And every time you honor it,
you reclaim your life from the machinery of urgency
and return it to the spaciousness of soul.

Pause & Remember

The Four-Second Return

A practice in sacred interruption

Before your next action—
sending an email, making a decision, speaking—
pause for just four seconds.

Let the breath come and go naturally.
Ask softly, *What is true right now?*

Let the impulse to rush rise—and don't follow it.
Simply stay.

Then choose, from presence—not from pressure.

Do this once a day. Or once an hour.
Each time, you deepen your capacity to lead from being
rather than habit.

You don't have to do more.
You only have to *begin within.*

———

*When your eyes are tired the world is
tired also. When your vision has gone
no part of the world can find you.*
—David Whyte

Space between

4 Being as Ground

> To be rooted is perhaps the most important and least recognized need of the human soul.
> —Simone Weil

THERE IS A PLACE BENEATH EVERY NAME you've carried.
Beneath the effort.
Beneath the story.
Beneath the mask and the memory.

It doesn't rise or fall with your circumstances.
It doesn't argue or perform.
It just *is*.

This is being.
Not the idea of being. Not the performance of calm.
But the actual experience of what remains when there's nothing left to hold up.

You don't create this state.
You return to it.
Or more precisely: you realize you never left.

What if you are not the wave, but the ocean?

Most of the time, we identify with what is moving—
our thoughts, our emotions, our roles, our tasks.

But you are not the movement.
You are the field the movement moves through.
You are the awareness that holds the storm, not the
storm itself.

Being is not passive.
And it is the most stable thing there is.

It is the part of you that doesn't flinch.
That doesn't react.
That simply watches—gently, without agenda.

And from that ground, real action can arise.

Action as expression, not escape

When you act from anxiety, the action carries it.
When you act from stillness, the action is stillness in motion.

You don't need to get still so you can act better.
You get still so that your action becomes honest.

From being, doing becomes natural.
Effortless, not because it's easy, but because it's aligned.

Being as Ground

This is not about detachment or inaction.
This is about moving from the source, not the surface.

Resting as wholeness

Most rest is a pause between efforts.
But this rest—this *resting as being*—is different.
It is not recovery. It is return.

You do not rest because you've earned it.
You rest because it is your nature.
Because wholeness isn't something you arrive at—
it's something you remember.

In being, nothing is missing.
There is no urgency.
No need to hold yourself together—because you were
never apart.

This is where leadership becomes luminous:
when it rises not from force, but from the quiet clarity of
someone who has come home to themselves.

Sit as the Mountain

A practice in resting as wholeness

Sit quietly.
Feel your body's weight. Let it drop into the earth.
Imagine yourself as a mountain—still, rooted, vast.

Let thoughts come and go like weather.
Let emotions move like clouds.
But you—the mountain—do not move.

Ask gently:
What if nothing is wrong?
What if I don't need to shift anything to be whole?

Let the question dissolve. Let presence deepen.
Stay as long as you like.

You don't have to fix the landscape.
You only need to remember you are the ground beneath it.

---

*We are all filled with a longing for the wild. There are
few culturally sanctioned antidotes for this yearning.
We were taught to feel shame for such a desire. But
the truth is that the soul doesn't want to be fixed, it
wants to be seen.*
—Clarissa Pinkola Estés

5 The Nature of Truth

> *Those who know do not speak.*
> *Those who speak do not know.*
> —Lao Tzu

TRUTH DOES NOT SHOUT.
It doesn't rush to explain or insist.
It doesn't seek validation.

Truth simply *is*.

It doesn't need to convince you.
It doesn't punish disbelief.
It is not fragile.

When you encounter it—not the idea of it, but the direct felt presence of it—you know.
Not because it fits a belief, but because it dissolves the need for one.

Truth is not belief. It is being.

Belief comes from the mind's hunger for certainty.
It selects, defends, repeats.
It creates identities out of opinions.

But truth does not rely on belief.
It doesn't depend on argument.
It doesn't tremble under scrutiny.

Truth is what remains when the noise settles.
It is not added—it is revealed.

Direct knowing

There is a kind of knowing before thought.
Not a concept. A resonance.

You've felt it.
A moment when something enters your awareness
fully formed, beyond logic.
It doesn't convince you. It *reminds* you.

This is direct knowing.
It comes not from thought, but through presence.
It doesn't need defense.
It's already whole.

Letting paradox be

Truth is rarely tidy.
It arrives in paradox
in tensions that don't cancel each
other but complete each other.

Freedom and responsibility.
Action and rest.
Being and becoming.

The mind wants to choose.
The soul holds both.

The leader does not collapse into either/or.
They widen to include both/and.

This is not indecision.
It is depth.

Truth doesn't need your defense. Just your presence.

Truth is not a slogan.
Not a performance.
Not something to wield against others.

It is something to stand in.
Quiet. Steady.

The leader rooted in truth doesn't persuade.
They resonate.

Others feel it—not because of what is said,
but because of what is silently lived.

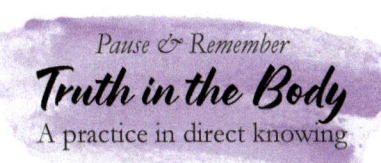

Pause & Remember
Truth in the Body
A practice in direct knowing

Sit quietly. One hand on your heart, one on your belly.
Breathe slowly. Arrive.

Bring to mind a statement you want to believe is true.
Say it softly within: *"This is true."*

Now feel.
Not think—*feel.*
Is there openness? Tightness? Resistance? Expansion?

Then release the statement.
Sit in the silence beneath language.
Let truth find you.

Over time, the body becomes a tuning fork.
You begin to *feel* truth before you try to prove it.

Let this be your compass.

———

> *When the heart is ready for fresh*
> *innocence, it finds a mirror where it*
> *least expects.*
>
> —John O'Donohue

Truth

6 *The Codes Within*

*Do you have the patience to wait till your
mud settles and the water is clear? Can you remain
unmoving till the right action arises by itself?*

—Lao Tzu

THERE ARE TRUTHS THAT CAN'T BE TAUGHT.

They do not arrive through effort.
They cannot be captured in language.
They move more like weather than instruction—
passing through, reshaping you.

But they are there.
Quiet. Radiant. Already inside you.

You've felt them in the way a hawk's call pierces your chest.
In the way a poem rearranges your breath.
In the way you've known something was true
long before you could say why.

These are not ideas.
They are Codes—imprints of your original creation.
Not to be decoded. But remembered.

They do not live in the mind.
They live in the field of being.

Inner architecture is not built. It is revealed.

We've been taught to build ourselves.
To stack identity. To assemble value.
To shape meaning through knowledge.

But the soul does not build.
It *reveals*.

The Codes within you are not waiting to be figured out.
They're waiting for you to stop trying to figure things out.

They don't arrive when you push.
They unfold when you pause.

There is nothing passive about this.
It's not disengagement. It's devotion.

The Codes are invitations from your deeper intelligence,
whispering:
You already know. You just stopped listening.

Receiving without needing to understand

The mind wants comprehension.
The soul wants resonance.

Not everything that moves you can be explained.
Not everything that heals you needs to be understood.

You may cry at a line of poetry without knowing why.
You may feel lit up by a color, or cracked open by a
stranger's gaze.

That's not confusion.
That's memory.

The Codes speak in symbol, dream, music, metaphor.
They bypass the intellect because they do not belong to it.
They belong to the part of you that *knows before it knows*.

Trust this.

Living transmissions

Some truths arrive as information.
Others arrive as transformation.

The deepest ones come through *presence*—not performance.
They transmit not from mind to mind, but from being
to being.

A tree.
A silence.
A sentence spoken from the center of someone's soul.

These are living transmissions.

They do not teach you what to do.
They remind you what you are.

This is the leadership the world aches for:
not those who have answers,
but those who can transmit truth through their *way of being*.

You are not here to decode life.
You are here to let life speak through you.

The Codes are not outside you.
They are the intelligence of your own unfolding.
Not demanding, but waiting.
Not loud, but precise.

Let them rise.

Pause & Remember

Open Listening
A practice in receiving the codes

Sit in silence. No agenda. No goal.
Place one hand over your heart.

Ask softly:
What wants to speak to me now?
Not from outside. From within.

Listen—not with your ears, but with your whole being.
A word might come. An image. A sensation. Or silence.

Don't analyze. Don't grasp.
Just *receive.*
Let the signal come like weather—passing through, shaping you gently.

Repeat often.
The more you listen, the more you hear.
The more you trust, the clearer the signal.

> *If the doors of perception were cleansed, everything would appear to man as it is—infinite.*
> —William Blake

響

Resonance

7 *Expression without Performance*

> *I want to be with those who know secret things or else alone.*
> —Rainer Maria Rilke

THERE IS A KIND OF EXPRESSION THAT EXHAUSTS.
It demands attention.
It seeks approval.
It performs its own worthiness.

And there is another kind of expression—
one that doesn't try, doesn't push, doesn't prove.

It simply *reveals*.

When expression arises from being, it carries no tension.
It doesn't seek confirmation.
It flows from what is true, not what is strategic.

This is the beginning of soulful leadership.
Not speaking *to be heard*,
But speaking *because something real wants to be shared*.

Expression is not performance.

You have been trained to perform.

To curate your presence.
To filter your truth.
To edit yourself in real-time.

This is not weakness.
It is adaptation—learned over years of sensing what is safe,
what is likable, what is rewarded.

But performance disconnects you from presence.
And leadership without presence becomes mimicry,
not embodiment.

When you lead from performance, your energy is split:
Part of you is doing the work,
and part of you is watching to see how it's being received.

That fracture costs you your wholeness.

To express is to reveal what is already true.

You don't need to perform your insight.
You only need to speak from the place where insight lives.

You don't need to convince others you're clear.
You only need to *be clear*, and let clarity do the work.

True expression does not come from crafting the
perfect message.
It comes from *allowing yourself to be seen.*

Even if you tremble.
Even if it's imperfect.
Especially then.

Because when you stop hiding, others feel less alone in
their own becoming.

Leading without needing to be followed

The most powerful leaders
are not the most followed.
They are the most *free.*

Free from image.
Free from control.
Free from the need to be
someone other than they are.

When you no longer lead to be followed
you are trustworthy.
You no longer try to pull others into your orbit.
You simply radiate—and those who are ready
find their own path home.

You do not need to brand your soul.
You need to be in such integrity with it that your presence
becomes its own invitation.

This is expression without performance.

Embodying what is already true

You are not here to impress.
You are here to embody.

You are not here to dim your light until it's palatable.
You are here to let it move freely—awkwardly, beautifully, in
its own rhythm.

Your presence, when real, does more than words ever can.
It tells the silent truth: *I am not performing. I am here.*

And that is what the world is starving for.

Pause & Remember
Speak from the Center
A practice in revealing without proving

Before a conversation, pause.
Place a hand over your chest. Breathe into your heart.

Ask yourself:
What is true for me right now?

When you speak, don't try to say it perfectly.
Just say it truthfully.
Without framing. Without apologizing.

Let silence follow your words.
You don't have to fill it.

Let yourself be seen.
Not as a performance, but as a presence.

The flute of the infinite is played
without ceasing, and its sound is love.
—Kabir

表

Authentic expression

8 The Courage to Be Misunderstood

Letting go of needing to be accepted to be authentic

> *It takes two to speak the truth: one to speak, and another to hear.*
> —Henry David Thoreau

THERE IS A QUIET COST TO TRUTH:
You will not always be understood.

You may be misread, dismissed, judged.
You may speak from the deepest place in you
and be met with silence—or worse, resistance.

This is not failure.
This is freedom doing its sacred work.

Because when you begin living from your essence,
you step out of the scripts others expect.

You stop performing the role.
You start becoming the real.

And the real does not always fit the picture.

The need to be understood is a form of safety.

From early on, we learn to adapt.
To shape ourselves into what will be accepted.
To smooth the edges of truth so we can stay close to love.

But often, that love required our distortion.

So we began to choose belonging over truth.
Agreement over authenticity.
Safety over self.

And yet—something in us never forgot.

In this moment you remember:
Belonging that requires you to betray your truth isn't belonging.
It's exile dressed up as connection.

Not being understood is not the same as being wrong.

When you are rooted in your own knowing,
you no longer need others to echo it back to feel whole.

You understand this:
Truth does not depend on consensus.

Sometimes, the clarity that moves through you
is meant to create space, not comfort.
It is meant to clear the air—not to be applauded.

To be misunderstood does not mean you failed.
It often means you stopped betraying yourself.

Facing the fear of freedom

Freedom is not always easy.
It can feel like loneliness.
It can feel like walking without the map you used to rely on.

But eventually, you realize:
What you feared would isolate you
is the very thing that connects you to life in its wholeness.

You begin to lead—not because everyone agrees,
but because you're no longer hiding.

You begin to speak—not to be accepted,
but because silence has become a greater betrayal than risk.

And that is courage.

Speaking truth without force

You don't have to make others understand you.
You don't have to argue your clarity into their frame.

You only need to stand in what is real—
softly, steadily, without apology.

Truth, when spoken without force,
becomes a kind of offering.

Not a demand.
Not a performance.
Just a quiet light, placed gently on the table.

You don't need to explain the light.
You only need to let it shine.

Pause & Remember
The Unfolded Yes
A practice in being seen without shrinking

Recall a time when you were misunderstood—but remained true.
Close your eyes and return to that moment.

Feel what rose in you. The ache. The doubt.
And also the knowing.

Say softly, to yourself:
Even if I am misunderstood, I choose to remain aligned.

Feel that alignment in your body.
Let it anchor you. Let it be enough.

This is not defiance.
This is dignity.

———

*I wish I could show you, when you are
lonely or in darkness, the astonishing
light of your own being.*

—Hafiz

勇

Courage

9 Leadership as Spaciousness

Experiencing trust, clarity, and emergence

> *Surrender is not about breaking something down, but about opening up.*
> —Marianne Williamson

TRUE LEADERSHIP IS NOT ABOUT CONTROL.
It is not about directing, solving, or filling the space.
It is about **experiencing** the space that is already here—and choosing to lead from that awareness.

Spaciousness isn't something you create.
It is something you **remember**.
It is the natural field beneath all performance, all posturing, all pretense.

The more deeply you rest in presence,
the more space becomes available for others to return to themselves.

You do not lead by pushing.
You lead by *being*.

From control to coherence

Control is noisy. It micromanages. It forces form.
It works hard to make things align.

But alignment doesn't come from control.
It comes from coherence.

When your words, presence, and actions rise from truth—
not from effort, not from performance—
you become coherent.

And coherence is magnetic.

It's not something you project.
It's something others *feel* in your presence.

They don't follow you because you're loud.
They attune to you because something in them *remembers itself*.

This is not persuasion.
It's resonance.

Spaciousness is not passive—it is power in its natural state.

To experience space is to return to what has always been present.
It is to drop beneath the surface noise
and let truth emerge *on its own terms*.

It takes courage not to fill the space.
It takes trust to stay aligned when clarity hasn't yet taken form.

But this is where leadership begins to transform.

Not by speaking over silence,
but by *being the silence* that allows real clarity to rise.

Not by guiding others into your image of truth,
but by offering a field in which truth becomes visible.

Making room for others to be whole

You don't have to inspire anyone.
You don't have to teach them who they are.

You only have to be so *aligned with your own being*
that others feel safe remembering theirs.

Leadership is not about being important.
It is about being *essential*—present, attuned, and undistracted.

When you are deeply present,
others don't feel observed.
They feel seen.

And in that seeing,
they start to soften,
to sense,
to return.

Leadership as a field, not a force

You are not the source of truth.
You are the space where truth is *felt*.

Your leadership is not the fire.
It is the hearth.

It is the still center others can lean toward
when the world feels fragmented, frantic, or false.

This is what soulful leadership does:
It doesn't *create* spaciousness.
It *experiences* it, and in doing so,
allows others to experience it too.

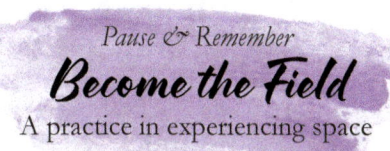

Pause & Remember
Become the Field
A practice in experiencing space

Sit or stand in quiet awareness. No task. No fixing.
Feel the space around you—not mentally, but bodily.

Soften your breath.
Let your awareness widen to include the silence.

Ask:
What alignment wants to reveal itself here?

Do nothing. Just be with what is.
Experience the space as alive, as intelligent, as enough.

This is not preparation.
This is presence.

———————

Be still and know that I am.
—Book of Psalms 46:10

Field of presence

10 *On*
Alignment

The invisible integrity of truth in motion

> *In silence, essence speaks to us of essence itself and asks for a kind of unilateral disarmament, our own essential nature slowly emerging as the defended periphery atomizes and falls apart.*
>
> —Rumi

ALIGNMENT IS NOT ABOUT PERFECTION.
It's not about getting everything "right."

It is a state of coherence—
where your thoughts, your actions, your words, your way of being are *rooted in the same ground.*

It is integrity—not as morality, but as wholeness.

You know it the moment you feel it.
There is no tension. No spin.
Nothing to manage. Nothing to protect.

There is simply: *yes.*
The quiet yes of the body,
of the breath,
of the truth that needs no rehearsal.

Alignment is being in right relationship—
with yourself.

When you are aligned, you are not trying to convince yourself.
There is no internal negotiation, no push or pull.
There is spaciousness.
There is clarity.

You are not fighting your own knowing.
You are following it.

You are not seeking validation.
You are resting in presence.

Alignment is not static. It moves.
It is less like a fixed position and more like **attunement**.
You adjust. You listen. You return.

Again and again.

The body knows.

Alignment is not something you figure out.
It is something you *feel*.

The body registers alignment before the mind can explain it.
It feels like ease, even when the choice is hard.
It feels like breath deepening, shoulders softening, spine rising.
It feels like truth moving through you without resistance.

When you override it, you know.
Something tightens.
Something disconnects.

The body always tells the truth—quietly, precisely,
without fanfare.

Misalignment is not failure. It is feedback.

You will lose alignment. Often.

That is not weakness.
That is rhythm.

Misalignment is not a verdict.
It's an invitation to return.

Not through force.
But through listening.

What feels off is not a flaw.
It's a signal.

Leadership begins here:
not in constant correctness, but in courageous returning.

Alignment is the origin of trust.

When your inner and outer match—people feel it.
They may not know why they trust you.
But they do.

Because you are not split.
Because your presence is clear.
Because your words are not decoration—they are reflection.

Alignment is the most subtle and powerful leadership there is.
It cannot be faked.
And it cannot be missed.

Alignment is a form of love.

It is the choice to no longer abandon yourself.
To no longer outsource your authority.
To no longer perform peace while holding tension inside.

To align is to honor the truth of this moment
as it moves through *you*.

And to let that truth guide your next breath,
your next word,
your next step.

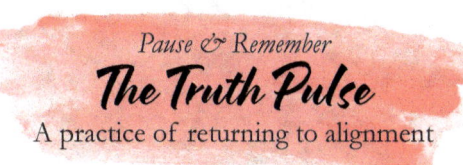

Pause & Remember
The Truth Pulse
A practice of returning to alignment

Sit. Breathe.
Ask yourself gently: *Am I aligned right now?*

Don't answer from the mind.
Let the body speak.

If you feel misalignment—tightness, resistance, performance—pause.
Ask: *What wants to be seen? What wants to be felt?*

Do nothing with it yet. Just name it. Feel it.
The return begins here.

This is the leadership beneath all leadership:
to be aligned,
even in the unseen.

———

We can make our minds so like still water that beings gather about us to see their own images, and so live for a moment with a clearer, perhaps even with a fiercer life because of our quiet.

—William Butler Yeats

整

Alignment

11 *The Weight of Holding On*

When attachment is a disguise for love

> *You only lose what you cling to.*
> —Buddha

THERE'S A CERTAIN ACHE THAT LOOKS LIKE CARE.
It wears the name of love, but tastes like fear.
You don't mean to grip. You only want to keep what
once steadied you:
a name, a role, a gaze that said, *I see you.*

But you cannot build stillness out of grasping.
And you cannot stay open when your hands are full of
yesterday.

Attachment is not a flaw.
It is tenderness that forgot how to trust.
It is memory performing as presence.
It is devotion wrapped in a quiet plea: *please don't change.*

But change is the soul's native language.
And love—true love—doesn't resist the river.
It floats with it.
It blesses the motion.
It knows that nothing real is ever truly lost.
Only transformed.
Only returned in new form.

The soft grip of longing

You didn't choose to cling.
You chose to remember what made you feel whole.
The way their eyes softened when you spoke.
The way a title steadied your spine.
The way a dream once mirrored your own becoming.

But memory is not a place to live.
It is a place to bow to.
And bowing is different from binding.

We hold onto things long after they've stopped holding us.
Not because we're weak, but because we're human.
Because we fear the blank space that letting go might reveal.

But that space?
That's where the soul breathes.

Letting go without leaving

You do not need to let go all at once.
You do not need to exile the past to be free of it.

You need only loosen.
Gently. Reverently.
As one loosens a thread—not to unravel the fabric,
but to find the place where it no longer needs to hold so tightly.

Letting go is not abandonment.
It is an honoring.
It is a soft return to the truth
that you are not what you carry.
You are what remains when you set it down.

What happens when you loosen

Loosening isn't loss.
It's remembrance.

The breath before the letting go.
The stillness that arrives
when you stop rehearsing how to hold what no longer
holds you.

What leaves was never the root.
Only the branch.
Only the shape truth wore for a time.

When you loosen, you don't fall apart.
You fall into space.
And space is not emptiness.
It is the room where what's real can return.

Sometimes there is grief.
Not for the thing itself—
but for the part of you that thought you couldn't live without it.
And sometimes there is silence.
A holy hush.
The kind that makes you listen more closely than you ever have.

This is not collapse.
This is the soft architecture of freedom.

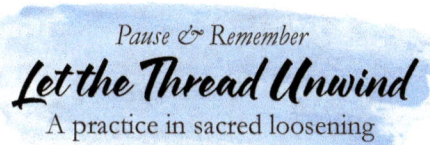

Pause & Remember

Let the Thread Unwind

A practice in sacred loosening

Sit in stillness.
Let your breath find its rhythm.
Bring to heart something you're holding onto—tight, silently, still.

Whisper:
Thank you for what you gave me. You don't have to stay.

Exhale.
Not to release, but to remember that you already have.

Rest in the space that remains.

You do not need to make sense of this.
You only need to feel the breath return to your hands.

You are not the grip.
You are the grace beneath it.
You are not the story.
You are the silence between its lines.

Love was never meant to be caged.
It was meant to move.

And so were you.

The only way to make sense out of change is to plunge into it, move with it, and join the dance.

—Alan Watts

12 *The Shape of Fear*

Turning toward what trembles

Fear is a natural reaction to moving closer to the truth.

—Pema Chödrön

FEAR IS NOT THE PROBLEM.
Forgetting who you are in the presence of fear—
that's where the ache begins.

Fear doesn't always come loudly.
Sometimes it arrives in silence.
A hesitation.
A sudden desire to wait.
A breath that won't go all the way in.

It says, *don't move yet.*
Don't speak.
Don't be seen.
It tells you safety lives in shrinking.

And for a while, it works.
But only by making you disappear.

The moment before the step

There is always a moment.
A pause.
Just before the words rise,
just before the truth breaks the surface.

And in that moment, fear comes.

Not to stop you.
But to ask:
Are you willing to stay open while this shakes you?
Are you willing to speak, even if your voice trembles?
Are you willing to remain visible—not perfect, but real?

That is the beginning of leadership.
Not moving without fear—
but moving *with* it.
As if fear is not a wall,
but a wind.

The body knows before the mind

Fear speaks in sensation before it ever speaks in thought.
A tightening in the chest.
A pulling away.
A thought that says, *Maybe later.*

But if you listen gently—
not to the story,
but to the space underneath—
you will hear something else.

A pulse.
A longing.
A whisper that says, *This matters.*

The closer you come to what is real,
the more fear tries to protect the shape you've outgrown.
Not because it's cruel.
But because it remembers how you once survived.

Fear is not the enemy.
It is a memory.
And memory does not need to lead—
it only needs to be seen.

Becoming spacious enough

You do not need to fight the fear.
You do not need to force your way through.
You only need to widen.
Just enough to stay.

There is a part of you that is not afraid.
It doesn't resist the trembling.
It doesn't need the answer.
It simply holds space—
soft, strong, still.

Soul of a Leader

You are that space.

You are the room fear moves through.
Not the one who must become smaller to survive it—
but the one who becomes larger to include it.

This is what it means to lead from presence:
To remain whole, even while afraid.
To act from truth, even when your hands are shaking.

Pause & Remember
Stay with the Shaking
A practice in becoming the space

Sit quietly.
Let your body arrive.

Bring to mind something that brings fear near.

Notice where it lives in the body.
Don't fix. Just witness.

Breathe into that place.
Not to remove it—just to stay
with it.

Say softly:
I can be with this. I don't have to be without it.

Stay.
Even for a breath longer than usual.

That breath is a doorway.

---

*Forget safety. Live where you fear
to live. Destroy your reputation.
Be notorious.*
—Rainer Maria Rilke

Reveal

13 The Lie of Not Enough

Seeing through the root illusion

> *You cannot buy the revolution.*
> *You cannot make the revolution.*
> *You can only be the revolution.*
> —Ursula K. Le Guin

BENEATH THE STRIVING,
Beneath the Polishing,
Beneath the Ache to Lead well,
There is often a quieter belief,
almost too familiar to notice:

"I am not enough."

Not wise enough.
Not clear enough.
Not awake enough.
Not worthy enough to rest.
Not broken enough to deserve healing.

This belief is so embedded, we don't question it.
We build our lives around it.
We call it humility. Or motivation. Or being realistic.

But it is none of those things.

It is a misunderstanding.
A trance.
A spell so old we've forgotten we're under it.

The myth of deficiency

The world taught you to measure yourself.
To earn worth.
To become acceptable.

And so, naturally, you believed:
If I just become *more*—more generous, more evolved, more capable—
then I'll be enough.

But the soul doesn't measure.
It doesn't grade.
It doesn't wait for some imagined future version of you.

It simply rests in what is.
It is never outside itself.

When we return to that way of seeing,
the myth of not enough begins to dissolve.

Presence undoes the illusion.

You don't have to fight the belief.
You don't need to argue with it.
That only gives it more energy.

You simply have to *see it*,
meet it with awareness,
and stop acting as if it's true.

When you sit in the presence of that old voice—
when you no longer resist or obey it—
something deeper opens.

A quiet remembering:
This voice is not presence.
This fear is not a fact.
This belief was never true.

You were never meant to prove.

What if the self you've been trying to earn
has always been here?

What if the wholeness you seek
is not a reward,
but your original condition?

This doesn't mean you stop growing.
It means you stop growing from fear.

You shift from striving to unfolding.
From proving to revealing.
From performing your worth
to resting in it.

The body remembers.

You may not believe it yet. That's okay.
Belief is not required for truth to work on you.

Truth is a frequency.
And when your system is ready,
it will begin to resonate.

The body often remembers first.
In a single breath. A tear. A softening.
You'll feel it:
You don't have to keep earning your place in life.

You're already here.
And you belong.

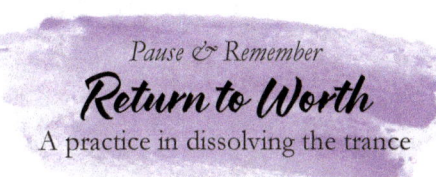

Pause & Remember
Return to Worth
A practice in dissolving the trance

Sit in stillness.
Let the breath come naturally.

Place a hand on your heart. Say softly, inwardly:
Even here, I am welcome.
Even now, I am enough.

Let the voice of doubt rise if it needs to.
Don't argue. Just witness.

Stay. Breathe.
Let truth reveal itself—not as thought, but as space.

You don't have to fix the voice.
You only have to stop following it.

That is the beginning of freedom.

You do not have to be good. You do not have to walk
on your knees for a hundred miles through the desert,
repenting. You only have to let the soft animal of your
body love what it loves.

—Mary Oliver

委

Surrender

14 The Generosity That Is

The unending stream beneath perception

> *I slept and dreamt that life was beauty.*
> *I woke and found that life was duty.*
> *I acted, and behold, duty was joy.*
> —Rabindranath Tagore

THERE IS A GENEROSITY THAT IS NOT A GESTURE,
not a giving *to*—but a giving *through*.

A generosity that is not effort, but essence.
Not a virtue, but a truth.
Not a choice, but a current.

This generosity flows, always.
Even when we don't notice it.
Even when we feel empty, tight, afraid.

It is not based on how full you feel.
It is based on the fullness of what you are.

Generosity as a condition of being

You are not separate from the stream.
You *are* the stream.

What flows through you when you are still enough to feel it—
that quiet warmth, that impulse to include, that soft yes—
is not something you manufacture.

It is the native rhythm of reality.
It is life loving itself through you.

When you withhold, it hurts.
Not because you're doing something wrong,
but because it goes against your design.

This includes how you treat yourself.
Self-generosity is often the most neglected form of flow—
the ability to extend tenderness inward, to speak to yourself
with the same warmth you offer others.

You are part of the stream. You are not its exception.

You are the opening.

So many of us believe we must accumulate before we give.
More energy. More clarity. More time. More love.

But generosity doesn't come *after* you are ready.
It *makes* you ready.
It opens the door that fear tries to close.

The soul is not a reservoir.
It is a river.

You are not here to hoard goodness.
You are here to let it pass through freely.

Even your pain, when honored, becomes part of that flow.
Even your silence can be generous—if it comes from presence,
not withdrawal.

And especially—your self-forgiveness, your pauses, your soft
boundaries—these are not indulgences. They are offerings.
They are generosity in its most intimate form.

Letting life give through you

Generosity is not a performance of kindness.
It is the transmission of coherence.

It's the way your listening softens a room.
The way your stillness steadies a storm.
The way your presence tells the quiet truth:
You are safe here. You are not alone.

You do not need to craft this.
You only need to stop resisting what is already moving through you.

When you live as the opening,
you begin to feel it:
There is always enough.

And that includes enough for you.
Enough time to rest.
Enough compassion to fall apart.
Enough trust to stop pretending.

Pause & Remember

Open Hands, Open Heart
A practice in becoming the flow

Sit quietly.
Place your hands palms-up on your lap.
Let your body soften. Let your breath find you.

Ask inwardly:
Where have I believed there is not enough?
Let the answers come—without fixing, without shame.

Now ask:
What is already flowing through me, right now?
Notice—even if it's subtle.

Finally, turn the same generosity inward.
What do I need that I haven't allowed myself to receive?
Let that receiving begin now, even in stillness.

There is nothing missing.
Only places you have not yet allowed the stream to move
freely.

Everything is gestation and then bringing forth.
To let each impression and each seed of a feeling
come to completion wholly in itself,
in the dark, in the unspeakable, the unconscious,
beyond the reach of one's own understanding,
and with deep humility and patience to wait for the hour
when a new clarity is born: this alone is what it means
to live as an artist—in understanding as in creating.

—Rainer Maria Rilke

15 Loving the Human You Are

Everything belongs

> Ring the bells that still can ring.
> Forget your perfect offering.
> There is a crack in everything.
> That's how the light gets in.
>   —Leonard Cohen

YOU'VE MOVED THROUGH REMEMBERING, forgetting, alignment, courage, truth, stillness, space.
You've looked into the mask, the mirror, the myth of not enough.
And now, there's just this:

Can you love the one who has walked the path?

Not the ideal. Not the integrated version.
Not the one who always listens to truth and acts with grace.

But *this* one.
The one who loops back.
The one who hides sometimes.
The one who cares so deeply it hurts.

This is the one worth loving.

Not because they got it right—
but because they are *real*.

You are not here to be perfect.

The soul has never asked you to get it all right.
Only to *show up*.

Only to stop abandoning yourself when things get messy.
Only to remember that worth was never a contest.

To love the human you are
is to be willing to live in full contact with life—
the pain, the beauty, the longing, the breath.

To stop performing healing
and start trusting wholeness.

Tenderness is a form of power.

You've likely been told that to lead is to be strong, clear,
unwavering.

But real leadership—soulful leadership—is wildly human.
It trembles. It pauses. It doubts. And then it breathes.

The most powerful presence
Is the one that doesn't hide its humanness.
That lets the cracks stay open,
so the light can keep getting in.

Loving the human you are means leading from tenderness,
not pretending you're above it.

And that tenderness—given first to yourself—
is what frees others to stop pretending too.

No part of you is in the way.

This is the most radical thing:
There is no part of you that is an obstacle to your becoming.

The grief. The doubt. The pieces you were told to clean
up before being seen—
they all belong.

Nothing has to be healed before you are whole.
Nothing has to be finished before you are real.

This is not about loving yourself as a project.
It's about loving yourself as presence.

You are not meant to become someone else.
You are meant to become *fully here.*

Pause & Remember
Full Welcome
A practice of belonging to yourself

Sit in stillness. Place your hand on your chest.
Breathe into whatever part of you feels most human
right now—
the ache, the shame, the longing, the joy.

Say inwardly:
You are welcome here.

Repeat it slowly.
Not to change anything.
To *include* it.

**Let the boundary between "what's lovable" and "what's
not" dissolve.**

There is no part of you that has to earn your love.
Only parts waiting to be included in it.

> *You were born with wings, why prefer
> to crawl through life?*
>
> —Rumi

Afterword

A Hand Extended

THIS IS NOT THE END. This is the path.

You were never meant to walk alone.
This book was never meant to be a finish line.

It's an open field.
A quiet rhythm.
A shared remembering.

If this journey resonated, softened something,
reminded you of what you already are—
you're warmly invited to stay connected.

Not to keep learning.
To keep **listening**.

To join others who are also practicing the path—
the pause, the return, the imperfect beauty of showing up from
truth.

You can join us at www.soulofaleader.net/discover
Or simply return to any page in this book.
Truth doesn't expire.

Let's keep walking each other home.

Acknowledgments

THIS BOOK COMES FROM JOY AND SUFFERING. I acknowledge the importance of all experiences as required steps to the place where this book can be shared.

I have been blessed with many teachers who were there at the perfect time. They've had different faces, and each of them offered reflections that were just right, showing me a clearer view of myself, even those I rejected. Their spirits are present as I write, like an audience waiting for the curtain to rise.

I mention them by first name, Orrie, Jeanne, Pearl, Helen, Niles, Steven, Richard, Terry, William, Andrew, Prim, James, Jim, Betty, Donovan, Jack, Jean, Mary, Karl, Jay, Ed, Tommy, Leslie, Patrick, Seth, Laura, Andy, Rachael, Russell, Layna, Peter, Muktananda, Cherie, Fred, Steve, Jo, Bob, Glen, Ann, Al, Jeff, Art, Richard, Will, Stephanie, Chris, Tom, Merle, Bill, Pete, David, Lynn, Jason, Pat, Doris, Sherry, Michael, Gabriel, Bijan, Kamran, Vincent, Rigel, Nicholas, Lisa, Jennifer, Maryanne, Ursula, Doug, Sarah, and Rubi.

One relationship has always reflected the source of the heart that beats in this book. This relationship started when I was a teenager and flowered into marriage. Then, divorce shattered it, only to be rekindled into the life we now share. Beth is the one who always reminds me that love is always there, in everyone and everything. Her zest for life and gratitude fill me with wonder and inspiration. Her encouragement, confidence, care, and reflection nurture my soul.

References

FOR THOSE WHO FEEL THE CALL to explore more deeply the sources of the quotations used in this book, I share this list of references.

Tao Te Ching — Translated by Stephen Mitchell
Harper Perennial Modern Classics, 1988

New and Selected Poems, Volume One — Mary Oliver
Beacon Press, 1992

Parable of the Talents — Octavia E. Butler
Seven Stories Press, 1998

Memories, Dreams, Reflections — C. G. Jung
Recorded and edited by Aniela Jaffé
Vintage Books, English edition, 1963

"Sweet Darkness" (from *The House of Belonging*) — David Whyte
Many Rivers Press, 1996

The Need for Roots: Prelude to a Declaration of Duties Towards Mankind — Simone Weil
Translated by Arthur Wills
Routledge, 2002 (original French publication, 1949)

Women Who Run with the Wolves: Myths and Stories of the Wild Woman Archetype — Clarissa Pinkola Estés
Ballantine Books, 1992

To Bless the Space Between Us: A Book of Blessings — John O'Donohue
Doubleday, 2008

The Marriage of Heaven and Hell — William Blake
Originally published 1790
Often reproduced by Dover Publications, various editions

The Book of Hours — Rainer Maria Rilke
Translated by Anita Barrows and Joanna Macy
Riverhead Books, 2005

Songs of Kabir — Kabir
Translated by Rabindranath Tagore
Macmillan, 1915

A Week on the Concord and Merrimack Rivers — Henry David Thoreau
Ticknor and Fields, 1849

The Gift: Poems by Hafiz, The Great Sufi Master — Translated by Daniel Ladinsky
Penguin Compass, 1999

References

A Return to Love: Reflections on the Principles of a Course in Miracles — Marianne Williamson
HarperOne, 1992

Consolations: The Solace, Nourishment and Underlying Meaning of Everyday Words — David Whyte
Many Rivers Press, 2015

The Celtic Twilight: Faerie and Folklore — W. B. Yeats
Macmillan, 1893 (numerous reprints; Dover Publications edition, 2003)

The Wisdom of Insecurity: A Message for an Age of Anxiety — Alan Watts
Pantheon Books, 1951

When Things Fall Apart: Heart Advice for Difficult Times — Pema Chödrön
Shambhala Publications, 1997

Feeling the Shoulder of the Lion: Poetry and Teaching Stories of Rumi — Translated by Coleman Barks
HarperOne, 1991

The Dispossessed: An Ambiguous Utopia — Ursula K. Le Guin
Harper & Row, 1974

Dream Work — Mary Oliver
Atlantic Monthly Press, 1986

Stray Birds — Rabindranath Tagore
Macmillan, 1916

Letters to a Young Poet — Rainer Maria Rilke
Translated by Stephen Mitchell
Vintage Books, 1986

"Anthem" (from *Selected Poems 1956–1968*) — Leonard Cohen
Viking Press, 1968

The Essential Rumi: New Expanded Edition — Translated by
Coleman Barks with John Moyne
HarperOne, May 28, 2004

About the Author

THOMAS WHITE HAS LIVED THE VERY path this book invites. As a CEO, founder, and advisor to organizations around the world, he knows the outer shape of leadership well. But the inner path—the one beneath achievement and identity—brings alive his purpose.

His journey blends decades of leading with a deep practice of listening: to truth, to presence, and to what remains when striving falls away. *Soul of a Leader* is both a reflection and a revelation—born not from theory but from a life lived in the loop of forgetting and remembering.

www.ingramcontent.com/pod-product-compliance
Lightning Source LLC
Chambersburg PA
CBHW071332130626
46556CB00004B/1869